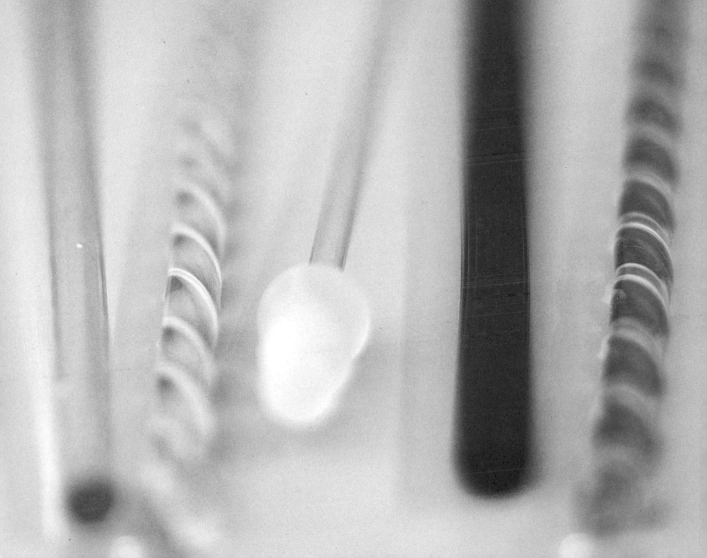

coolers
and summer
cocktails

coolers
and summer cocktails

elsa petersen-schepelern

photography by
james merrell

RYLAND
PETERS
& SMALL

Art Editor **Penny Stock**

Assistant Designer **Lucy Hamilton**

Editor **Elsa Petersen-Schepelern**

Creative Director **Jacqui Small**

Publishing Director **Anne Ryland**

Production **Kate Mackillop**

Food Stylist **David Peacock**

Stylist **Wei Tang**

Author Photograph **Francis Loney**

My thanks to my sister Kirsten, Nowelle Valentina-Capezza, Peter Bray and Sheridan Lear for their enthusiastic help and advice – to Marwan Badran and the troops at Euphorium Restaurant in Islington for lending us the restaurant as the setting for the photographs – and to Lucy Hamilton for her presentation design. Thanks also to Tim and the summer gathering at Le Mandorle in Tuscany for their critical assessment of Morocco Mary.

First published in Great Britain in 1998
by Ryland Peters & Small
Cavendish House, 51-55 Mortimer Street, London W1N 7TD

Printed and bound in Hong Kong by Toppan Printing Co.

ISBN 1 900518 56 2

A CIP record for this book is available from the British Library

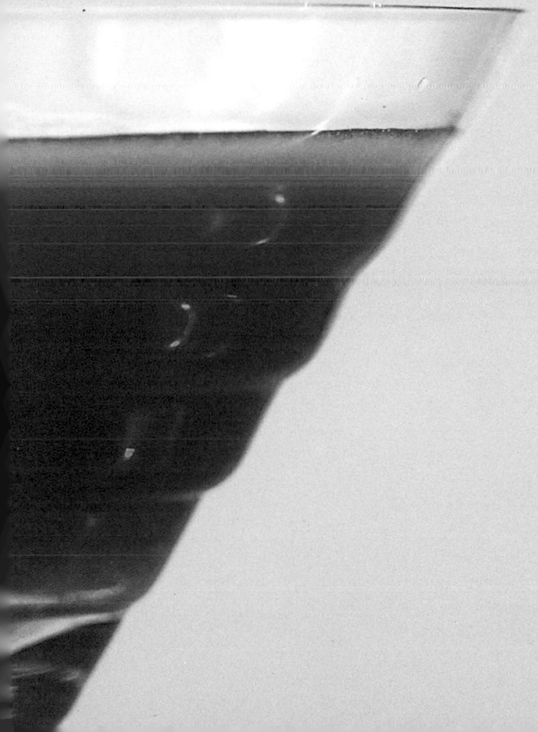

coolers
and summer
cocktails

Drinks in the garden, lunch on the deck, barbecues, tennis parties and sunbathing – all essential summer pastimes requiring the drinks in this book. You'll find recipes for children and adults, drinks with and without alcohol, cocktails for one, or for casts of thousands (or quite a few, anyway!)

Old-fashioned lemonade and ginger beer are great for hot summer days, while cocktails like Mint Mojito and Negroni should definitely wait until the sun is over the yard-arm! But you can always make them longer and less heady by adding a mixer and serving them in a long glass.

The book includes recipes you won't find in other books – try, for instance, Morocco Mary, a Bloody Mary made with harissa paste, the gorgeous Moroccan spiced chilli purée. Most ingredients used in the book are widely available, in shops selling wine and spirits, as well as in specialist grocers, good delicatessens and many of the larger supermarkets.

coolers and summer cocktails 6

Moroccan mint tea is served hot in tiny
engraved and gilded glasses – it's the
perfect finish to a spicy Moroccan meal
and helps oil the wheels of conversation
in countless tea shops across the
country. I like it equally well chilled and
iced as a cool summer drink.
I prefer to make it in a cafetière, then you
don't have to bother with straining or
fishing out the leaves. If you don't have a
cafetière, you can also make it in a big
jug or teapot, then strain into a second
jug before chilling and serving.

moroccan iced mint tea

1 large bunch of fresh mint sprigs
boiling water, to cover
mint sprigs, to serve
sugar, to taste, served separately

Fill a cafetière with mint, pour over boiling
water and let cool. Push the plunger, then
pour the tea into a jug. Chill, then serve in
tea glasses with mint and a dish of sugar.
Serves 4–6

summer coolers

fresh homemade
ginger beer

This ginger beer is quicker than the traditional kind – which fills your cupboards with bottles that explode over the following weeks. I also think the taste is fresher and brighter. Don't peel the ginger if you're zapping it in a food processor – just chop it up roughly then pulse until well chopped. The skin will give the beer extra flavour.

125 g grated fresh ginger

zest and juice of 2 limes

2 cloves

200 g sugar (brown gives better colour)

Put all ingredients in a large cafetière or pitcher, pour over 1 litre boiling water, stir until the sugar dissolves. Cool, plunge or strain, then chill well. To serve, half-fill glasses with the mixture and top with soda water or fizzy mineral water.

Serves 4

apple
lemonade

This recipe is best made with cooking apples – they turn to delicious apple-flavoured foam when boiled. For a much quicker result, use fresh apple juice, omit the sugar, add the fresh lemon juice and fill with mineral water.

2–3 cooking apples, unpeeled, chopped into small pieces

sugar, to taste

juice of 1 lemon

fizzy mineral water, to serve

Put the apples in pan, cover with cold water, bring to the boil and simmer until soft. Strain, pressing the pulp through the strainer with a spoon. Add sugar to taste, stir until dissolved, then let cool.

To serve, pack a jug with ice, half-fill the glass with the apple juice, add the lemon juice and top with mineral water. Alternatively, serve in individual glasses.

Serves 4

a quick and **easy apple** drink

for children or grownups

jamaican iced ginger
sorrel tea

Jamaican sorrel is the flower of a native hibiscus, sold fresh or dried in Caribbean stores or in health food shops, where it is known as Red Hibiscus Tea. It's also known as 'rosella' in Australia and New Zealand, and is used to make jam. It's an unusual, sophisticated taste, and if you like vaguely bitter flavours, you'll love it!

1 tablespoon ginger purée

4 tablespoons dried sorrel flowers or hibiscus tea

4 tablespoons sugar

ice

a twist of lime

Put the first 3 ingredients in a cafetière. Pour over boiling water. Plunge when liquid is light purple, then cool and chill. Serve over ice with a twist of lime. To serve as a longer drink, top up with ginger ale, soda or mineral water. The cocktail below usually has lots of sugar, but I prefer it less sweet.
Serves 4–8

Variation:

Sorrel Rum Cocktail

Put 4 tablespoons dried sorrel, a curl of orange peel, 1 cinnamon stick, 6 cloves and 200–400 g sugar, in a cafetière, pour over 1.5 litres boiling water, stir well, then push the plunger. Add 2 extra cloves and a cinnamon stick to the top, cool and chill. To serve, pour over ice, then add a jigger of rum and a cinnamon stick for swizzling.
Serves 6–8

pineapple
strawberryade

A summer cooler that's simply the most glorious colour and tastes like heaven!

zest and strained juice of 2 lemons

strained juice of 2 oranges

1 medium pineapple, peeled and cored

2 tablespoons icing sugar, or to taste

10–12 ripe red strawberries

sliced strawberries or a curl of citrus peel, to serve

Put the pineapple, strawberries, lemon zest and icing sugar in a blender with about 125 ml iced water and zap until smooth. Add the orange and lemon juices and another 125 ml iced water. Taste and add extra sugar if necessary (depending on the sweetness of the fruit). Pour over a jug of ice and decorate with sliced berries and a twist of orange or lemon peel.

Serves 6–8

a gingery Caribbean variation on one

of the great **Indian classics**

mango
ginger lassi

This mango lassi is made with the Indian Alphonso – the world's greatest mango. If you can't find him fresh, purée any variety of sweet mango in a blender. The good-quality canned Alphonso mango purée sold by Asian grocers can also be used instead (and tastes spectacular).

250 ml Alphonso mango purée
250 ml low fat plain yoghurt
1 tablespoon ginger purée
crushed ice
1 litre Jamaican ginger beer

Put the first 4 ingredients in a jug and mix well (I used a pair of chopsticks). Top up with ginger beer and serve.
Serves 6–8 or more

cranberry
cooler

Cranberry mixed with citrus juice is a marriage made in heaven – the prettiest, cloudy pink. Try the soft version below, or the heady variation (right). To make the Carrot Cooler, use freshly-crushed carrot juice, which you can now buy in good sandwich bars, supermarkets and health food shops. Just make sure you buy the fresh kind – the canned or bottled kind isn't suitable.

crushed ice

1 cup cranberry juice

1 cup orange juice

sparkling mineral water.

a twist of orange peel, to serve

Fill a jug with ice, pour over the cranberry and orange juice, and stir well. Top up with sparkling mineral water and serve with a twist of orange peel.

Serves 1–2

Sea Breeze

Use grapefruit juice instead of orange, omit the mineral water and add 125 ml vodka.

Serves 2–3

Lime and Carrot Juice Cooler

Put 250 ml carrot juice in a cocktail shaker with the juice of 1 lime, crushed ice and 1 tablespoon ginger purée or juice from preserved ginger. Shake then strain into a long glasses packed with ice and serve with shreds of lemon zest.

A shot of gin or vodka turns this drink a real pick-me-up!

Serves 1

rhubarb berryade

Make this unusual, old-fashioned drink with pretty pink forced rhubarb for an utterly stunning colour, or add a dash of Grenadine to point up the colour.

500 g rhubarb, trimmed and sliced
2 tablespoons icing sugar
rind and juice of 1 lemon
6 strawberries
fizzy mineral water, to taste

Put the rhubarb in a pan with the sugar and cover with at least 1 litre of boiling water. Stew until the rhubarb is very soft. Add the strawberries and boil hard for about 1 minute, then strain into a jug and cool. To serve, pour into a jug of ice, stir in the lemon juice and top with mineral water.

Serves 4–8

Variation:

Orange and Rhubarb Tea
Another great drink to make with rhubarb! Stew 500 g rhubarb in a pan with 1 litre boiling water and the rind of a lemon. Strain, discarding the solids. Cool, chill, add 500 ml iced tea, the juice of 1 lemon and 1 orange and stir. Add 1 thinly sliced orange and serve with a dish of caster sugar, so everyone can sweeten to taste.
Serves 4–6

We've all had commercial lemonade, which is little more than fizzy sugar water. Real lemonade, on the other hand, is cool and refreshing and actually tastes of lemons. These recipes are good old-fashioned lemonades, taken from hand-written recipe books lent by aunts and grandmothers. It always reminds me of tennis parties, wicker chairs on the lawn, drinks in the cool shade of the verandah, and with lemonade served by my mother, the last woman in the world to own a parasol!

real lemonade

1 litre water

1½ tablespoons lemon juice

3–4 tablespoons sugar

a pinch of salt

ice cubes

mint leaves

a few slices of lemon

Boil the sugar and water for 2 minutes. Chill and add the lemon juice, then serve in a frosted glass pitcher with ice and mint and a few thin lemon slices floating on top.

Serves 2–4

citrus coolers

a delicious, old-fashioned drink,
great for **summer parties**

old-fashioned
orangeade

2 oranges, sliced and deseeded,
but unpeeled

1 lemon, sliced and deseeded,
but unpeeled

50 g sugar, or to taste

1–1.25 litres boiling water

Put the sliced oranges, lemon and sugar in a large jug, pour over boiling water, cover, cool and chill. Serve, strained over glasses of ice, with a curl of orange peel to decorate. Alternatively, double the quantity of fruit, peel the rinds, discarding any white pith. Put the rinds in a jug, sprinkle with 2 tablespoons sugar, then squeeze the citrus juices and add to the jug. Fill with boiling water and let stand until cool. Taste and stir in extra sugar if necessary. Strain into a jug of ice and serve in long glasses filled with more ice.

Serves 2–4

These old-fashioned drinks are not fizzy like modern soft drinks. For fizz, make a stronger mixture by decreasing the quantity of water, then serve the drinks topped up with fizzy mineral water or soda. We added fizz by serving through a Sodastream® machine.

Variation:

Granny's Orangeade

This variation is very similar, but tastes a little more 'orangy'. Peel the rind of 4 oranges, leaving the white pith behind. Put the rind into a jug with a little sugar, and add the juice of the oranges and 1 lemon. Pour over 1 litre boiling water, let stand until cool, strain and serve over ice. You can also use less water and add soda water or mineral water when serving.

Serves 2–4

These soothing, cooling old-fashioned drinks are incredibly easy to make since the invention of the cafetière – the coffee maker with the plunger. In Victorian times, platoons of kitchenmaids would boil up the lemon and barley, strain it through muslin into enormous pitchers, leave it to cool, then try to chill it with whatever technology was available in the Big House at the time. Lucky us – we have cafetières and ice. So much easier! The Apple Water variation is wonderful.

Variation:

Apple Water

Purée the juice and zest of ½ lemon, 3 cored, sliced apples and 1 tablespoon sugar in a food processor. Transfer to a cafetière and pour over 750 ml water. Cool, plunge and chill before serving.

lemon
barley water

2 tablespoons pearl barley

1.5 litres boiling water

grated zest and juice of 1 large, unwaxed lemon

2 teaspoons sugar

a curl of lemon peel

Put the barley in a pan, cover with the boiling water and simmer for 30 minutes. Strain into a cafetière, then stir in the sugar, lemon zest and lemon juice. Cool, plunge, chill, then serve over crushed ice, decorated with a curl of lemon peel.

Serves 2–4

indian fresh
lime soda

I have been to India many times, and it never seems to get any cooler! My favourite thirst-quencher – served everywhere from five-star hotels to village truck-stops – is this fresh lime soda, served either with salt or sugar (or, in my case, plain). You wouldn't think that salty drinks could be at all pleasant, but Indians serve fresh lime sodas and yoghurt lassi drinks with a pinch of salt, and they are incredibly cooling. Try it and see!

Surprisingly, the French variation, the Citron Pressé, is very similar. Lemon juice is squeezed into a glass, and served with a separate jug of iced water and a bowl of sugar. I think this is just the perfect cooler in the middle of a hard day's shopping in Paris!

1–2 limes
1 small bottle soda water
sugar or sea salt, to taste
crushed ice or ice cubes (optional)

Squeeze the juice from the limes into a tall glass. Serve with a bottle of soda water or fizzy mineral water, and small dishes of salt or sugar, according to taste. Crushed ice or ice cubes may also be added.
Serves 1

Variation:
Citron Pressé
Squeeze the juice of 1 lemon into a tall glass. Serve with a jug of iced water, a small dish of sugar and a long spoon.
Serves 1

pimms

This traditional English summertime drink is perfect for tennis parties and polo matches. When borage is in flower, freeze the pretty blue blossoms in ice cubes for out-of-season Pimms drinks. Allow 250 ml per drink, and at least 2 drinks per person if serving Pimms for a party and be prepared for repeat orders! But take care – this delicious cooler is very strong.

1 part Pimms
3 parts ginger ale, lemonade or soda
borage flowers
curls of cucumber peel
sliced lemons and sprigs of mint

Put all ingredients into a jug of ice and serve.
Serves 1 or a party

party drinks

mint mojito

The Caribbean and Central America have created some fabulous taste combinations, often based on rum. A Mojito is essentially a rum julep, and you can make it in the same way as the julep on page 52. However, being lazy, I like mine made in a blender, and just love the amazing colour produced by the blended mint leaves. Traditional recipes use soda water as a top-up, but I prefer fizzy mineral water. This is also great without the rum, but either way, it's a perfect summer cooler!

125 ml white rum
juice of 1 large lime
4 tablespoons icing sugar, or to taste
a large handful of fresh mint sprigs
ice cubes
soda water or fizzy mineral water
mint sprigs, to serve
a curl of lime zest

Put the rum, lime juice, sugar, 4 ice cubes, 125 ml mineral water and mint leaves in a blender and whizz. Strain into a jug, then pour into tall glasses packed with ice. Top with mineral water or soda water to taste, add lime zest and a sprig of mint and serve. To serve a larger number of people, increase the quantities accordingly, and instead of pouring into glasses, pour into a jug one-third full of ice, then top with mineral water and serve.

Serves 1-4

tropical
sangria

Spanish Sangria with a South American twist! Use any fruit, but include tropicals, like mango, pineapple or starfruit. Don't use any that go 'furry', such as melon or strawberries. This is great for a summer party in the garden, and you can produce a non-alcoholic kind for children and non-drinkers using ginger ale or lemonade instead of the champagne.

1 ripe mango, finely sliced
1 lime, finely sliced
1 lemon, finely sliced
½ pineapple, wedged and finely sliced
3 kiwifruit, sliced
1 starfruit (carambola), sliced
3 tablespoons caster sugar
1 bottle champagne

Slice the fruit into a punch bowl. Sprinkle with sugar and set aside for 30 minutes. Top with icy champagne just before serving.
Serves 4–8

Variations:

Quick Neapolitan Sangria
Half-fill a punch bowl with ice, add 1 bottle orange squash and 2 bottles light red wine.
Serves 8–12

Neapolitan Red Peach Sangria
Half-fill a punch bowl with ice, add 1 bottle light red wine, 250 ml peach nectar, mint sprigs and 1 sliced peach.
Serves 4

This punch – great for a party – is very strong, so if you want to give people more than one glass, make it gentler by adding a bottle or two of ginger beer, ginger ale or mineral water. If you can't find ginger wine, use dry sherry mixed with about 2 tablespoons ginger purée.

6 limes (3 juiced, 3 sliced)

½ bottle ginger wine

1 bottle vodka or white rum

sugar, to taste

3 lemons, sliced

1 starfruit, sliced

1 pineapple, cut lengthways into long wedges, then crosswise into triangles

sprigs of mint, to serve

mighty jamaican punch

Mix the lime juice, ginger wine and vodka or rum with the sugar until dissolved.
Fill a punch bowl with ice, add the sliced fruit and pour over the ginger wine mixture.
Stir well and serve with sprigs of mint.
Serves about 16–20

caribbean **tea** punch

Make this punch with a flavoured tea like Lapsang Souchong or Earl Grey. I make mine in a small cafetière so I can plunge the plunger as soon as the tea reaches the right colour – after 30 seconds to 1 minute, before the tannin is released. The scent of lemon mixes beautifully with the rich scent of rum. For parties, make a big pot of tea, mix with half its volume of rum. Sweeten and serve with mixers.

1 cup weak black tea

1 tablespoon caster sugar

crushed ice

125 ml dark rum or golden rum

peeled zest of ½ lemon

1 lemon slice (optional)

Stir the sugar into the hot tea. Let cool, then stir well. Fill a glass with ice, pour over the tea, stir in the rum and lemon zest, and serve with a slice of lemon.

Serves 1–2

Variations:

Mango Rum Punch

Mix 250 ml mango purée, 1 teaspoon lemon juice, a pinch of cardamom and 500 ml golden rum. Stir well, pour over ice and serve, topped with a few cardamom seeds. (For the best cardamom, crush 6 green pods in a mortar and pestle, extract the black seeds and discard the green pods.)

Serves 3–6

Planter's Punch

There must be hundreds of combinations for Planter's Punch, and their composition probably depended on where the planter lived – this one comes from sugar-growing areas such as Australia and the Caribbean. In a large jug, put 250 ml white rum, 250 ml pineapple juice (freshly crushed if possible), 250 ml mango purée or mango juice, the grated zest and juice of 1 large lime and a dash of Angostura Bitters. Stir and serve over ice, with a cinnamon swizzle stick.

Serves 3–6

the Caribbean is the source of some of **the greatest** rum cocktails

kumquat ratafia

Ratafias are simple to make – just fruits macerated in brandy. Serve as a small drink or topped up with mineral water.

kumquats (see method)
sugar (see method)
1 cinnamon stick
3 cloves
brandy (see method)

Fill a large preserving jar with kumquats that have been washed and pricked several times with a skewer or needle. Fill the container one-third full with sugar, add the cinnamon and cloves, fill with brandy and set aside for about 2 months. Serve the liquid as a liqueur, poured over crushed ice as a cocktail, or as a long drink with a mixer, such as mineral water, soda or lemonade. The fruit is wonderful sliced and served in fruit puddings, or pan-fried in butter and served with meat or game.

Makes 1 jar, about 1 litre

Variation:

Spiced Orange Ratafia
Grate the zest of 6 big oranges and squeeze the juice into a 2-litre preserving jar. Add 500 g sugar, 1 cinnamon stick and ½ teaspoon ground coriander. Stir until the sugar has dissolved and let stand for about 30–60 minutes. Pour over 1.25 litres brandy, cover with a lid and shake the jar. Set aside for 2 months, shaking the jar from time to time. Use as in the main recipe.

Thailand meets the South of France — with some **variations** from Southern Italy

mango kir

Thailand meets the South of France – or Southern Italy in the variations right! For the Mango Kir, use canned mango purée (preferably made from Indian Alphonso mangoes), or purée a fresh ripe mango in a blender with a little iced water and 1 tablespoon of lemon juice to help the mango keep its colour.
For a non-alcoholic version, replace the champagne with ginger ale.

500 ml mango purée
2–4 tablespoons ginger purée (optional)
250 ml crushed ice
ice-cold champagne (see method)

Zap the mango and ginger purées in a blender with the ice. To serve, half-fill each glass with the mixture and top with champagne. Omit the ginger if preferred.
Serves 6 or more

Rosa-frizzare

A refreshing combination from Southern Italy. Mix 100 ml Campari and 400 ml grapefruit juice in a jug. To serve, half-fill each glass with the mixture, add ice and top with champagne. For a special party, decorate with sprigs of mint.
Serves 6

Mandarin Fizz

Mix 1 litre mandarin juice and 250 ml Cointreau or Grand Marnier in a chilled jug. To serve, pour a little of the mixture into each glass, then top with champagne. For a single cocktail, omit the champagne and pour the fiery juice over ice.
Serves 12–16

Bellini Kir

Put about 2 tablespoons peach liqueur and some sliced peach in each champagne glass and top with iced champagne.
Serves 1 or many

The summery flavour of ripe red watermelon goes wonderfully well with the fresh, clean, lemony taste of gin. I grew up in the tropics, where there were lots of different watermelon varieties. The round ones with dark green skins and orange-red flesh were called sugar-melons, but the enormous torpedo-shaped ones with striped skins and pinky-red flesh were our favourites. The seed-free section in the middle of a melon is the sweetest, so if you're cutting pieces for a garnish, use this part.

2 very ripe watermelons, well chilled

2–4 cups gin (or to taste)

to serve:

crushed ice

sprigs of mint

watermelon triangles (optional)

watermelon
gin

Cut the watermelon in half and remove the rind and seeds. Whizz the flesh in a blender or food processor. If the mixture is too thick, add water. Pour into a jug, stir in the gin, and serve in small glasses with crushed ice, a sprig of mint, and a melon triangle.
Serves 4–6

Variation:
Lime and Watermelon Vodka
Substitute vodka instead of the gin, and stir in the juice of 2 limes.
Serves 4–6

negroni

One of the great classics – using
Campari, one of my favourite flavours –
a little bitter, a little sweet, a little smoky.
It's a stunning colour – serve it in
stemmed glasses, over ice, 'up with a
twist' as they say.

1 part Campari
1 part gin
1 part dry vermouth
ice
1 lemon slice or twist of lemon peel

Pour the first 3 ingredients into a glass, add
ice, stir, then decorate with a lemon slice or
a twist of lemon peel.
Serves 1

summer
cocktails

whisky **mac**

Utterly delicious for people who like their drinks spicy but not too sweet. For a weaker version, serve in a long glass and top up with a soft drink.

1 part whisky
1 part green ginger wine
ice
a curl of lemon peel
ginger ale or ginger beer (optional)

Shake the whisky, ginger wine and ice in a cocktail shaker. Strain into a small glass and serve with a curl of lemon peel.
Serves 1

Variation:
Whisky Sour
Shake 35 ml bourbon or whisky with the juice of half a lemon, then strain into a whisky sour glass.
Serves 1

Traditionally, a mint julep should be served in a silver or pewter mug, so the frosty surface isn't marred by finger marks, but a chilled glass jug, frosty highball glasses, and a drinking straw work just as well.

mint julep

3 tablespoons sugar syrup
24 mint leaves, torn, plus mint sprigs
1 teaspoon Angostura Bitters (optional)
375 ml bourbon
ice cubes

Muddle the sugar syrup in a tall glass with the mint leaves and bitters, if using. Stir in the bourbon. Pack a chilled pitcher with ice and mint sprigs then strain in the julep. Alternatively, pack tall glasses with ice, then pour over the julep. Serve with straws.
Serves 4

Variation:
Brandy Mint Julep
Use brandy instead of bourbon, and serve.
Serves 4

marvellous
margarita

Margaritas are my favourite cocktail – great but lethal when made properly – but sometimes almost totally without alcohol when ordered in a bar (probably a good idea!)
The usual way of serving margaritas is to rim the glasses with salt – this is optional, but I think that a twist of lime is absolutely crucial!
Some people also like a dash of sugar in this drink – though, in my opinion, this depends on the flavour of the limes.

Variations:

Frozen Margarita

In a blender, whizz 1 part tequila, 1 part Grand Marnier, 2 parts fresh lime juice, 2 parts ice and sugar to taste, then pour into ice-frosted, salt-rimmed glasses.

Serves 1

Cranberry Margarita

In a blender, whizz 1 part each of tequila, Cointreau and lime juice with 2 parts of cranberry juice and ice, and sugar to taste.

Serves 1

1 part tequila
1 part triple sec or other orange liqueur, such as Cointreau
2 parts fresh lime juice, thinned with water if preferred
crushed ice or ice cubes
a twist of lime, to serve

Shake or blend the first 4 ingredients, then serve with a twist of lime.

Serves 1

morocco mary

The absolutely best Bloody Mary you ever tasted! I promise you! I have served this recipe to Bloody Mary purists and it was a huge success. In trying to emulate my efforts, one particularly purist friend added the harissa paste to his regular spicy recipe and wondered why some of his guests looked decidedly overheated!

1 teaspoon harissa paste

juice of 2 limes

75 ml vodka

250 ml tomato juice

salt and freshly ground black pepper

ice

In a jug, mix the harissa, lime juice and vodka, then the remaining ingredients. Alternatively, zap the harissa in the blender with the tomato juice and lime juice, then pour into the jug, stir in the vodka, and add salt and pepper to taste.

Serves 1–2

Variations:

Traditional Bloody Mary

Mix 50 ml vodka with 125 ml tomato juice, the juice of 1 lemon, a dash of Tabasco sauce and Worcestershire sauce, and a pinch of celery salt. Stir well in a long glass with ice cubes and serve with a celery stalk.

Virgin Mary

Omit the vodka and proceed as above.

Serves 1

Daiquiris always look so festive, and you can change the fruit to taste: pineapple or banana are both great! I like to use golden rum because it has a better taste – but the colour will change somewhat.

frozen strawberry
daiquiri

juice of 2 limes

2 tablespoons icing sugar

125 ml white rum

6 strawberries

dash of strawberry liqueur (optional)

about 250 ml crushed ice

In a blender, zap all the ingredients until frothy, then pour into daiquiri glasses – preferably enormous!
Serves 2

Variations:
Lemon-Bacardi Daiquiri
In a blender, zap 3 parts Bacardi, 2 parts lemon juice, 1 part sugar syrup with ice.
Serves 4–5

Daiquiri Granita
In a blender, zap 25 ml sugar syrup, 75 ml lime juice, 350 ml rum, a dash of grenadine and 250 ml ice and serve in iced glasses. (Sugar syrup is 2–3 parts water, 1 part sugar, boiled for 2 minutes, then cooled).

ginger rum

Rum and ginger make a marriage made in heaven – the very essence of the tropics! Golden rum from Barbados is a wonderful compromise between the elegance of white rum and the power-flavour of my favourite dark rum. The result is a delightful golden colour.
Serve as a cocktail, or as a long drink with your favourite mixer to make a drink more or less sweet.

1 piece stem ginger, crushed to a purée

1 teaspoon ginger syrup from the jar

60 ml golden rum

1 tablespoon fresh lime juice

about 125 ml crushed ice or 6 ice cubes, plus extra, to serve

1 lime wedge

Crush the stem ginger to a purée with a fork, and scrape into a shaker. Add the ginger syrup, rum, lime juice and ice. Shake well, then strain into a glass filled with ice and garnish with a wedge of lime. Add extra syrup if you prefer a sweeter drink. Alternatively, zap in a blender, then strain over ice.
For a long drink, serve in a Collins glass topped with ginger ale or soda.
Serves 1

a wonderful, golden cocktail with the
zippy spice of ginger

I grew up in tropical Australia, with wonderful, fresh juicy ripe pineapples and sweet dark Bundaberg rum – in our view the finest of all rums. However, it isn't such a pretty colour when used with ingredients like these, so instead use a golden rum from Barbados or one of the other Caribbean islands. You could also use white rum, but it doesn't have the depth of flavour of the darker ones.

Australia, also produces some of the world's finest ginger, which is exported all over the world. In this recipe, use preserved ginger in sugar syrup, or make your own fresh ginger purée by zapping fresh ginger root in a blender with a little lemon juice. You can spoon it into an ice cube tray, freeze it and use a cube when you need it – in drinks, or cooking.

pineapple
rum

500 ml fresh pineapple juice
or 1 ripe pineapple, peeled and cored
2 tablespoons ginger purée
or 2 pieces preserved ginger and ginger syrup to taste
250 ml white rum or golden rum
ginger beer or ginger ale (optional)

Zap the pineapple or juice in a blender with the puréed ginger or ginger syrup. Strain into a tall jug of ice. Stir in the rum and serve immediately, or top with ginger ale or ginger beer. Alternatively, strain into tall glasses full of ice, and top with ginger ale.
Serves 4–6

Index

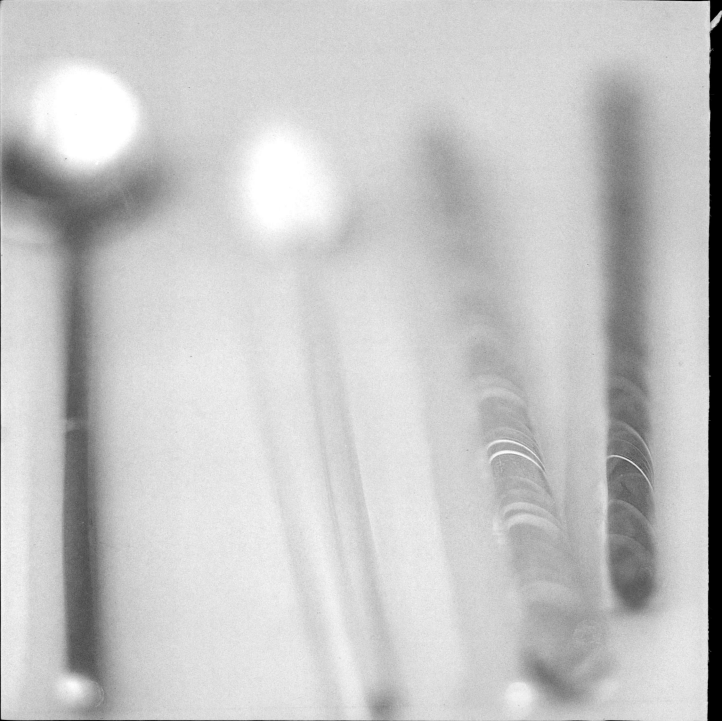